.

Origami

an illustrated
Teach Yourself Book

Illustrated Teach Yourself

Robert Harbin

Origami The art of paper folding

**Brockhampton
Press**

To Neal Elias and Fred Rohm

ISBN 0 340 16646 0
First published 1973

Copyright © 1973 Robert Harbin
Models by the author and Mrs Winifred Smith
photographed by Geoff Johnson
Line illustrations by Jane Harper

Printed in Great Britain by Fletcher & Son Ltd, Norwich

Contents

A short history of Origami   **10**

The essentials of Origami   **12**

International Origami symbols   **14**

Reverse folds   **16**

Feet   **18**

Bird's head   **19**

House   **20**

Boat   **23**

Salt cellar   **25**

Spanish box   **29**

Samurai hat   **34**

Sampan   **38**

Sanbow   **42**

Multiform   **47**

Bird base   **53**

Flapping bird   **60**

Pigeon   **63**

Frog   **67**

Penguins   **72**

Penguin   **75**

Tropical bird   **78**

Decoration   **80**

Ornithonimus   **84**

Swans   **88**

Books and materials   **91**

A short history of Origami

'Origami' (pronounced *or-i-gäm'e*) is a Japanese word which means paper-folding. The Japanese do not consider Origami to be an art form, but look on it rather as something which is an integral part of their culture.

Associated in the first instance with the making of intricate paper dolls, the designing of *Noshis* (folded tokens) and of attractive packaging, Origami has now become an accepted pastime for the young and an intellectual hobby for many adults.

In Japan, two great names dominate the Origami scene: Akira Yoshizawa and Okimasa Uchiyama. The genius of Yoshizawa has influenced most Japanese and Western folders.

Because of the sudden interest the West has shown in Origami, Japanese publishers have been quick to produce a flood of attractive books on the art, written in Japanese and English, many of which contain complete finished models pasted into the books themselves.

Although these Japanese books are a delight to look at, they fail in the object of teaching. Westerners do not easily follow diagrams, and the Japanese wrongly assume that their explanations are sufficient instruction for the beginner

Peter Van Note, of New York, who is a keen paper-folder has carried out some research into the origins of Origami and has the following observations to make:

'I recently acquired, by pure chance, a Japanese manuscript describing paper-folding according to the ancient practices. It was published about the same time as the Kan No Mado manuscript, but I have reason to believe that it illustrates the paper-folding of Japan's Heian Period (AD 782–1185).

'If this is proven true (and I believe it can be), then we have the earliest examples of paper-folding on record – about 1,000 years old.

'In the Japanese way of figuring time, the manuscript dates back to the middle of the Edo Period, which lasted from about the time England's Henry Hudson was sailing up the Hudson River (1607–11) to shortly after the American Civil War (1865).

'For what it is worth, here is a thumbnail outline of the history of Origami:

'Elaborate ceremonial paper-folding and simple "recreational" paper-folding – Heian Period.
'Water Bomb Base: probably used in the Heian Period for making ceremonial paper butterfly figures.

'Crane Base (Bird Base) : Edo Period, probably 1700s to mid 1800s.

'Frog Base : Late Edo Period, probably not before the 1800s.

'The above conclusions must necessarily be tentative but they are based on good evidence. It should be noted that the Heian and Edo Periods were times of peace and leisure in Japanese history, while the intervening four centuries were characterised by instability and bloody battle.'

Thank you, Peter Van Note!

The Spanish have been great paper-folders for many years, and the best Western results have emerged from Spain and the Argentine. You should watch out for names like Vicente Solorzano, Ligia Montoya, N. Doctor Montero and many more.

In Great Britain, things are beginning to happen these days and some fine originals are appearing. Look out for names like Eric Kenneway, Iris Walker, and Trevor Hatchett and Tim Ward.

By far the most exciting results are coming from America, and you will come across names like Fred Rohm, Neal Elias, Robert Neale, George Rhoads, Jack Skillman and many others, both male and female. Many books would need to be written to keep pace with the flood of originals coming from this source.

Mrs Lillian Oppenheimer, of New York, has devoted a great part of her life to stimulating interest in Origami, and to this end she runs an Origami Center in New York, and is the publisher of *The Origamian,* which keeps the dedicated enthusiasts in touch with current Origami happenings.

A British Origami Society has now been formed, and all enquiries should be addressed to:

The Secretary, British Origami Society,
193 Abbey Road, Warley, Worcs.

I am happy to include in this Illustrated Teach Yourself book some originals by contemporary folders from many countries, and to them I tender my grateful thanks.

I am grateful to Mrs Winifred Smith who helped with the folding and arrangement of models for photography.

The essentials of Origami

As you have elected to teach yourself Origami, by now you will be anxious to go ahead and start work on the models in this book. First, though, there is some helpful information to be considered, and the following essential instructions must be read carefully.

All the diagrams are clearly drawn, and contain helpful instructions and symbols to give you all possible help, and to explain the mainly standard models which bring you in touch with most of the Basic Folds.

A Basic Fold is a fold from which many models can be made. There are many Basic Folds, both ancient and modern, but this book will introduce you to just enough to give you a good groundwork on which to begin.

Notice how the instructions are placed close to the parts to be folded: 'fold this side down', and so on. The instructions are made to work for you.

Always fold carefully, accurately and neatly. If you fold carelessly, the result will be disastrous.

Study each diagram or photograph showing the complete folded model. Then, and only then, place your Origami paper in front of you and make your first fold.

When you make a fold, always crease the paper firmly with the back of your thumbnail. Good creases make folding easy and are an invaluable guide later in the model, when you are making a series of folds.

Pre-creasing is an important feature. Before you make a Reverse Fold, pre-crease the paper by folding the whole thickness before opening the paper and making the fold (see Reverse Folds).

Notice how paper coloured on one side is used to get the maximum effect for each model. The subject of paper is an important one. Origami paper (which is available from a variety of sources, some of which I have listed on page 91) should be strong, thin and suitably coloured. But if you cannot lay hands on special Origami paper, almost any paper may be used.

If you are instructed to use a square of paper, make sure that it really is square, and that a rectangle is a true rectangle. Most of the models in this book are based on squares of paper, but there is no regular rule about this, as all shapes of paper can be used, according to the model's needs. See, for example, the Ornithonimus.

Origami is not meant to be a simple art. To the expert, it is a challenge to the eye, the brain and the fingers, a wonderful mental and physical therapy.

When you fold the Decoration explained in this book, you will find that by altering this or that fold you can invent endless shapes. In fact, you can doodle for hours.

When you have mastered the Basic Folds, you will then

be equipped to produce figures and shapes of your own. Have something in mind, and then consider the best Base from which to start. You will notice that there are two different ways in which to make a Penguin. The Penguin seems to be a favourite subject and almost every folder has had a go at it.

Watch out for terms like Squash Fold. It is so named because you do just that — squash the part indicated so that the sides bulge and it flattens, in most cases symmetrically.

Study the Petal Folds, the Rabbit's Ears, and the various Bases, and try to remember what they are. If you get stuck, have a look at the Contents and refer to the page or pages concerned.

You will notice that certain procedures are used over and over again. You will soon get used to these and be able to carry them out automatically.

When you have folded everything in the first half of the book, you will find that more and more diagrams begin to appear on each page, and that the symbols begin to play a bigger part than the instructions.

Start at the beginning of the book and work your way slowly and steadily through. Do not attempt anything too difficult to start with, because this can only end in disappointment.

If you are making a long train journey, take this book with you, and fold a piece of paper to pass the time during your journey. Find a friend with the same interest and you will both pass many a happy hour.

For the rehabilitation of damaged hands there is nothing like Origami for making reluctant fingers come back to life.

Finally — take it slowly; fold carefully, neatly and accurately. And *start at the beginning*.

International Origami symbols

Study the symbols carefully; they take the place of instructions.

The symbols used in this book are based on Akira Yoshizawa's code of lines and arrows. Symbols must become second nature to you when folding, but you will find that they are easy to acquire.

The moment you see a line of dashes, you know that the paper must be Valley Folded along that line. When you see a line of dashes and dots, you recognise the sign for a Mountain Fold. To make a Mountain Fold, you naturally turn the paper upside down and make a Valley Fold.

Arrows show the directions in which you must fold: left, right, up, down, in front, behind, and into.

You will notice one arrow which shows that a drawing has been enlarged for clarity. Another arrow indicates that a model must be opened out (see Sidney French's Ornithonimus). My own special little black arrow indicates that you must sink, press, squeeze or push in at certain points.

The symbols are in fact self-explanatory. They are simple common sense and can be learnt in about ten minutes.

Try to use the symbols only and ignore explanations. This will help you when you come to read Japanese Origami books.

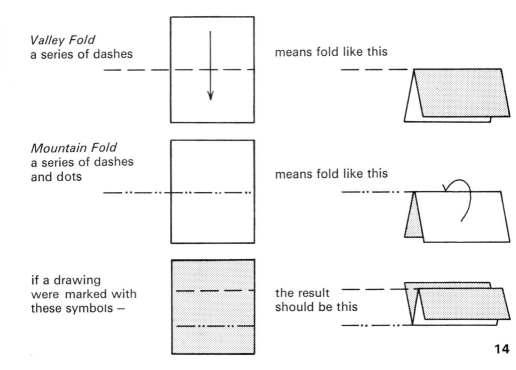

Valley Fold
a series of dashes

means fold like this

Mountain Fold
a series of dashes and dots

means fold like this

if a drawing were marked with these symbols —

the result should be this

when a drawing
is followed by
this little looped
arrow —

turn the model
over — so

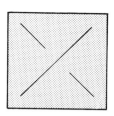

this black arrow

means push in

thin lines mean
creases

this symbol

means fold
over and over

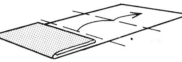

if a drawing is
marked like this —

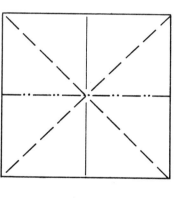

you make this
Water Bomb Base

if you turn this fold
inside out you will
get this
*Preliminary
Fold*

15

How to make Reverse Folds

Reverse Fold (1)

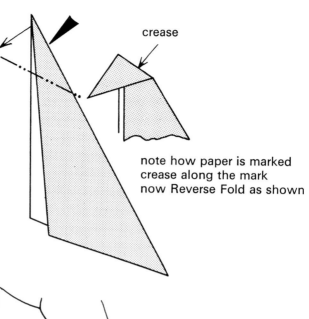

crease

note how paper is marked
crease along the mark
now Reverse Fold as shown

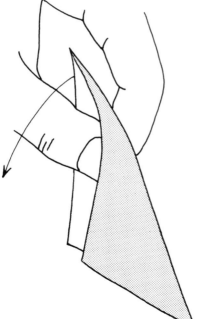

like this

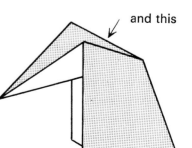

and this

crease

*n 'Outside'
Reverse Fold* (2)

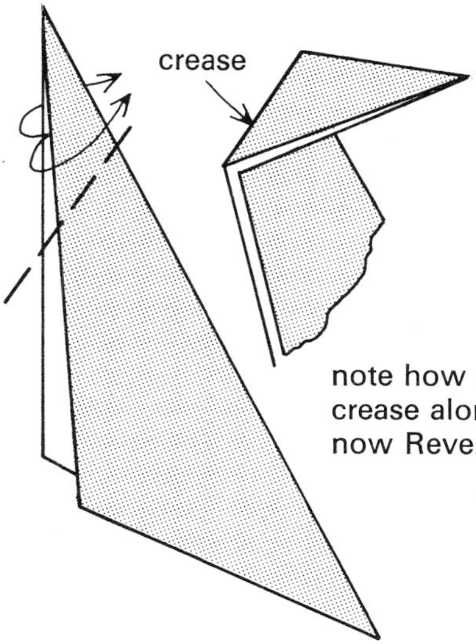

note how paper is marked
crease along the mark
now Reverse Fold as shown

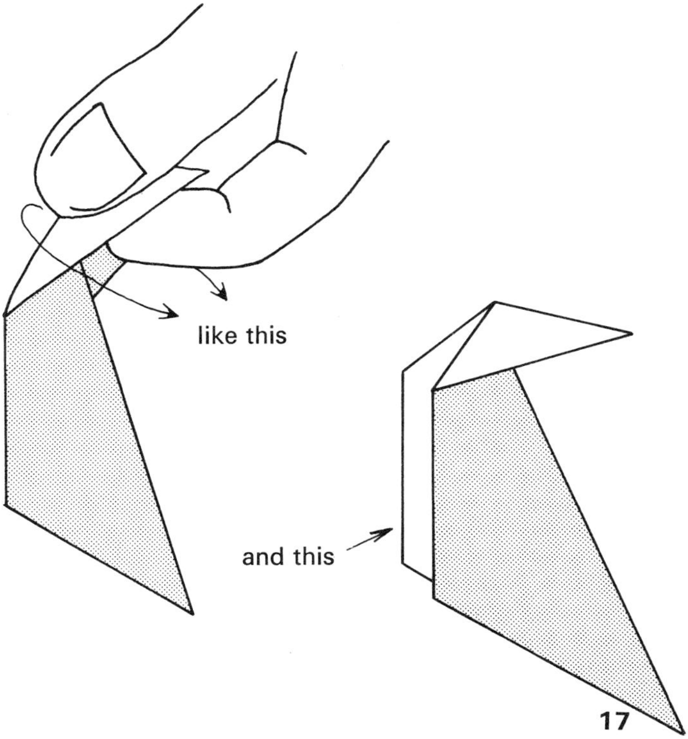

like this

and this

17

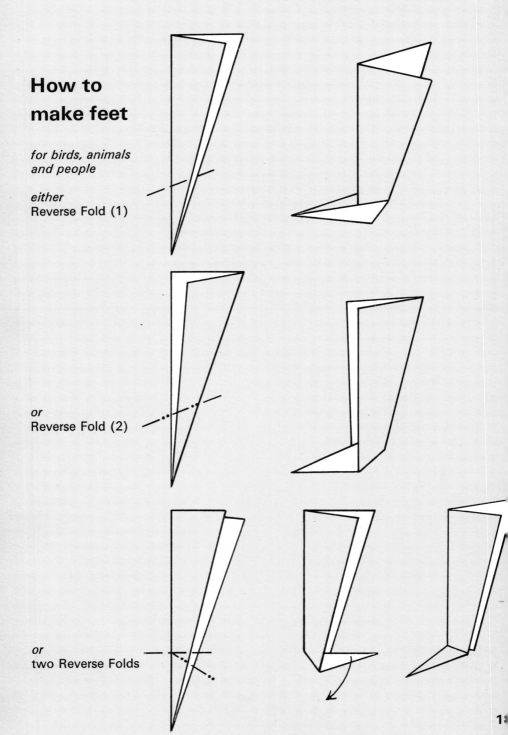

How to
make feet

*for birds, animals
and people*

either
Reverse Fold (1)

or
Reverse Fold (2)

or
two Reverse Folds

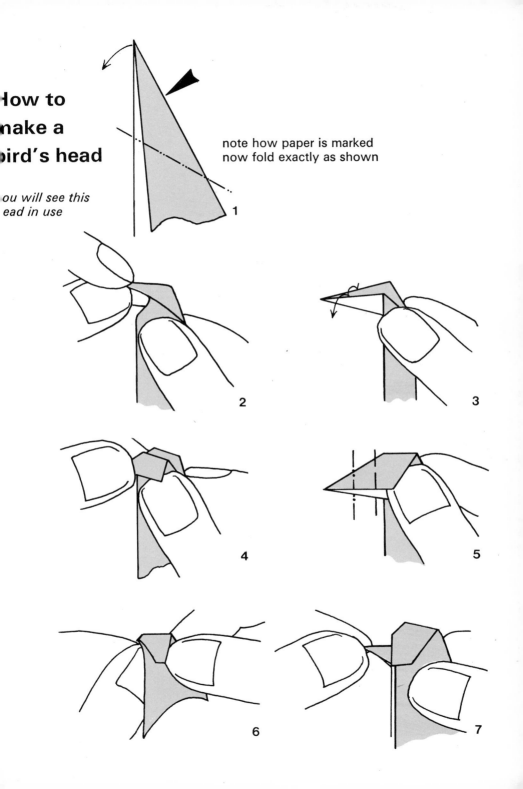

How to make a bird's head

You will see this head in use

note how paper is marked
now fold exactly as shown

1

2

3

4

5

6

7

House

This is a simple Japanese fold

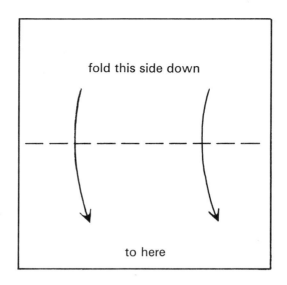

fold this side down

to here

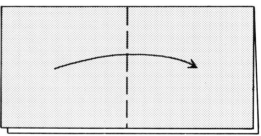

fold over

to here

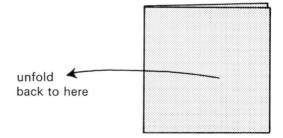

unfold
back to here

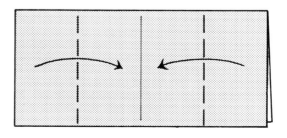

fold sides to middle

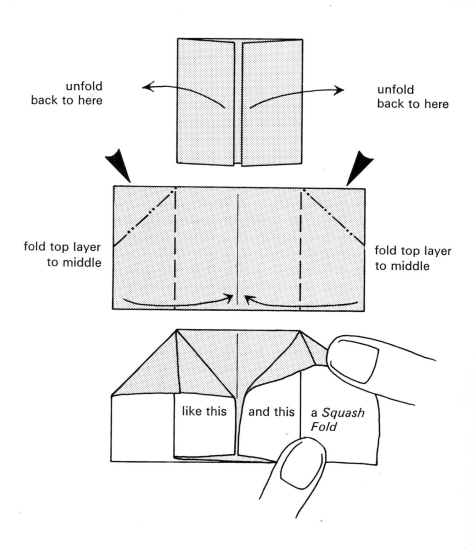

unfold
back to here

unfold
back to here

fold top layer
to middle

fold top layer
to middle

like this | and this | a *Squash Fold*

now draw doors and windows

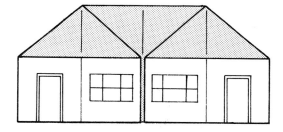

[*see photograph on next page*]

Boat

*Use a square
of paper*

First crease
along the middle

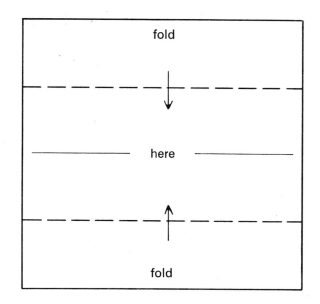

fold

here

fold

fold in half

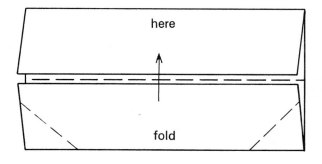

here

fold

now fold the
two corners up

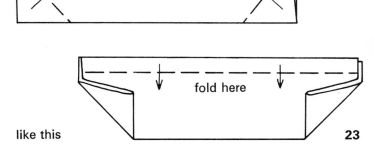

fold here

like this

23

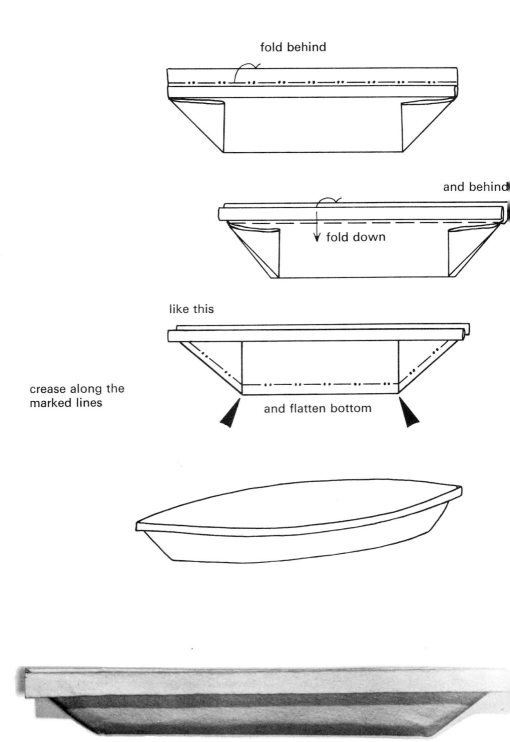

fold behind

and behind

fold down

like this

crease along the
marked lines

and flatten bottom

Salt cellar

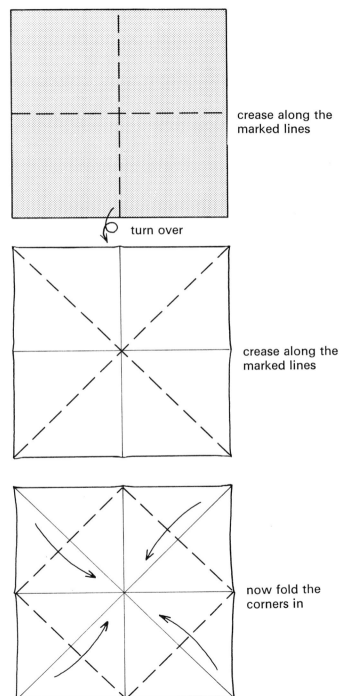

crease along the
marked lines

turn over

crease along the
marked lines

now fold the
corners in

25

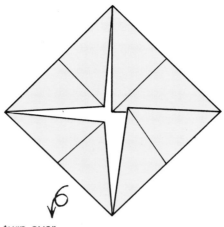

turn over

fold the corners in

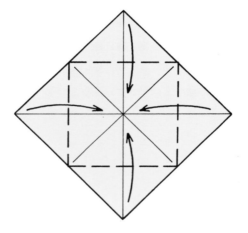

like this

enlargement

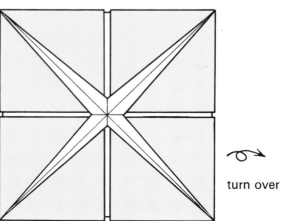

turn over

26

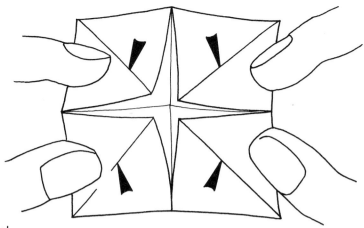

squeeze into shape

like this

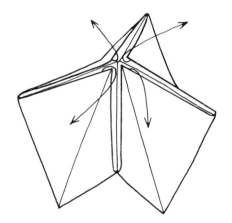

pull out the
four flaps

like this

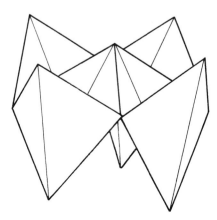

You can make a *colo*
changer by turning th
model upside down a
colouring the surface
in different colours.
With your fingers
underneath the flaps,
open and close the
model to show the
different colours

Spanish box

This fold is Spanish, originally Japanese

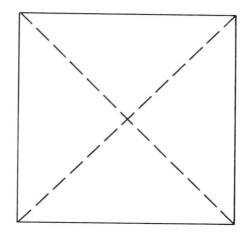

crease along the
marked lines

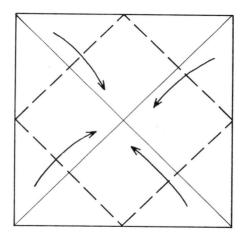

fold the
four corners
to the centre

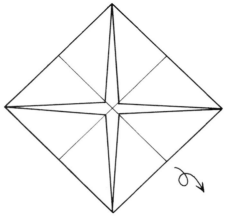

like this

turn over **29**

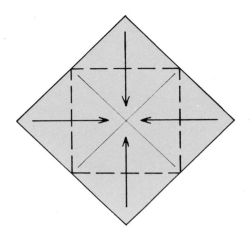

fold four corners
to the centre

enlargement

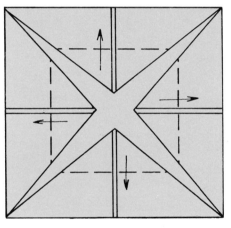

fold back the flaps
as shown

like this

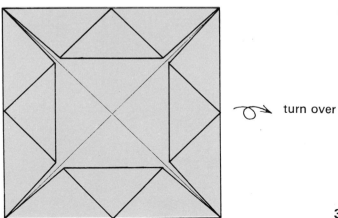

turn over

31

pleat flaps

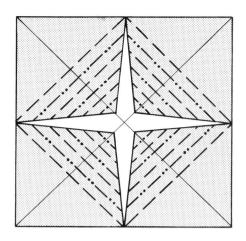

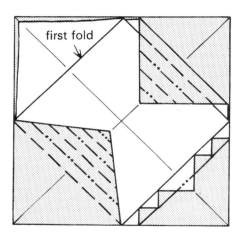

first fold

one pleat only

nearly complete

completed pleats

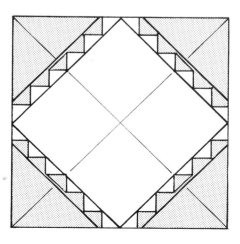

32

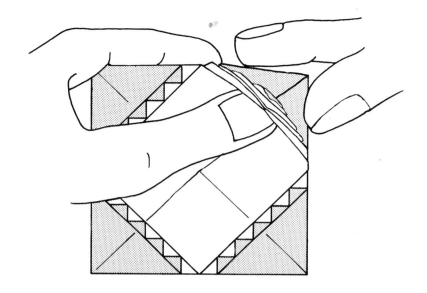

push left thumb into each
corner and press together
on the outside until the
fancy box is completed –
so

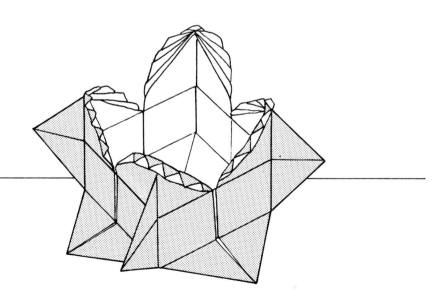

the box can be
filled with sweets

Samurai hat

*A traditional
Japanese fold*

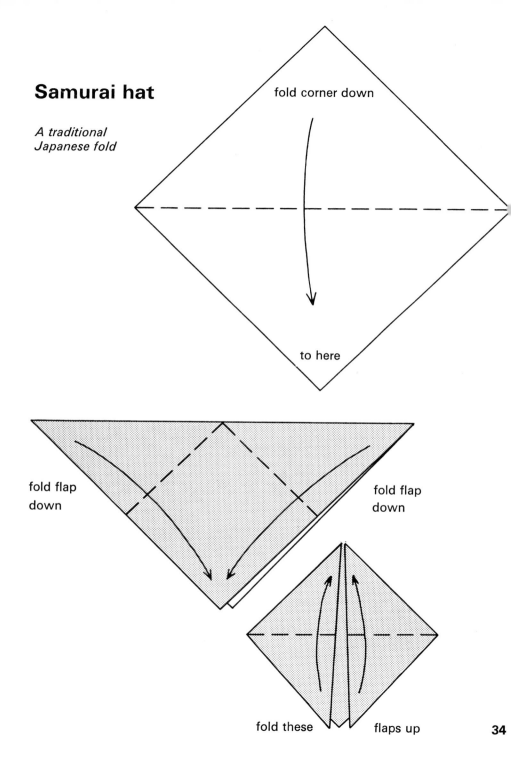

fold corner down

to here

fold flap
down

fold flap
down

fold these

flaps up

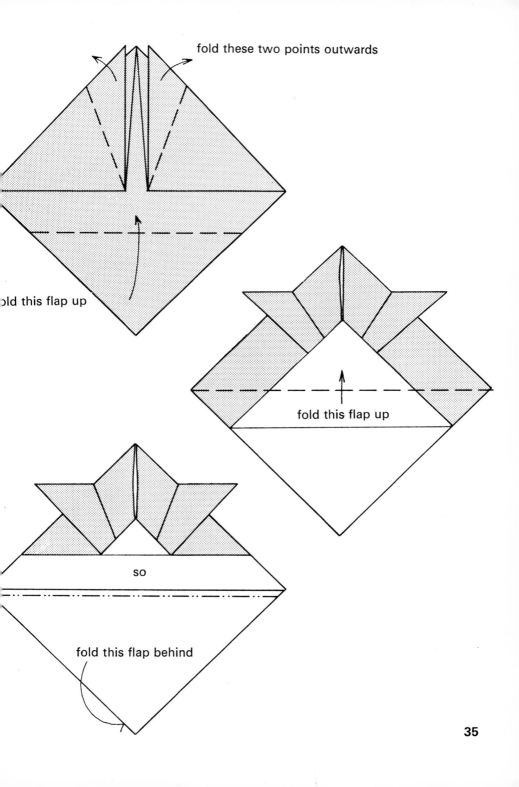

fold these two points outwards

fold this flap up

fold this flap up

so

fold this flap behind

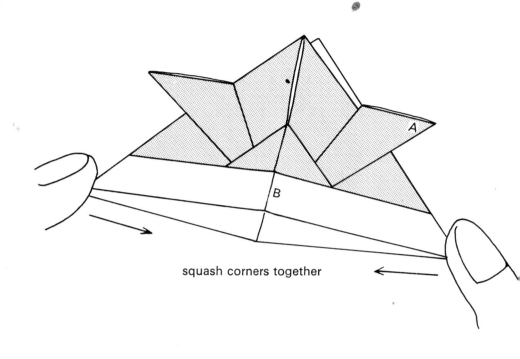

squash corners together

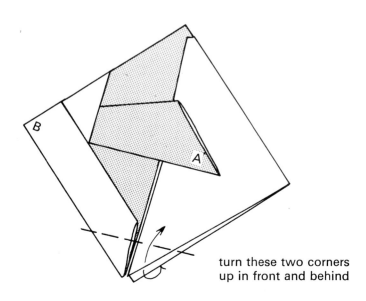

turn these two corners
up in front and behind

34

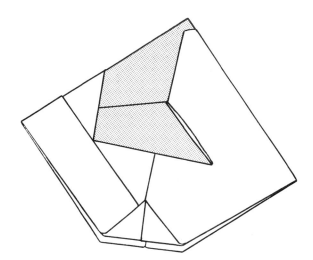

now open up again

a piece of paper 20 in.
square will make a hat
to fit your head

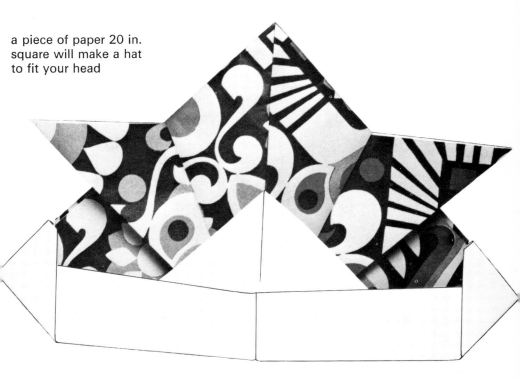

Sampan

*This fold is of
Korean, Chinese and
Japanese origin*

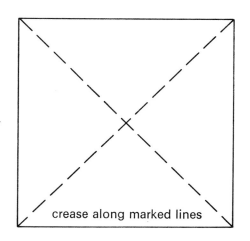

crease along marked lines

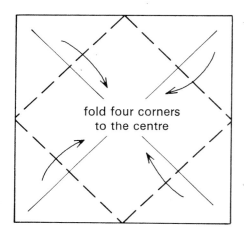

fold four corners
to the centre

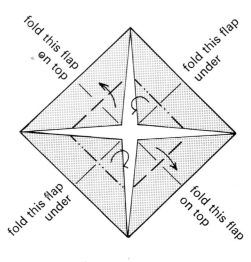

fold this flap on top

fold this flap under

fold this flap under

fold this flap on top

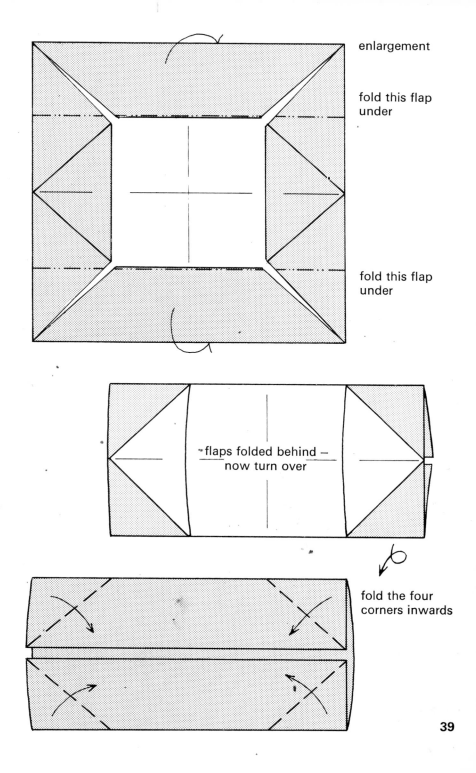

enlargement

fold this flap
under

fold this flap
under

flaps folded behind —
now turn over

fold the four
corners inwards

fold the four
corner flaps inwards

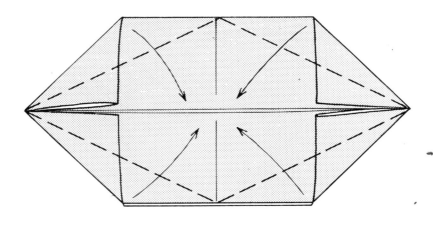

fold flap down

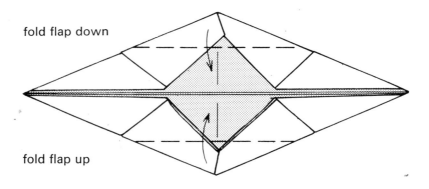

fold flap up

open up the middle

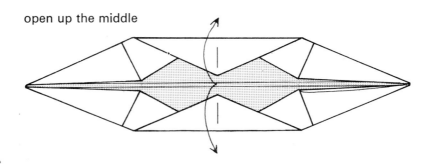

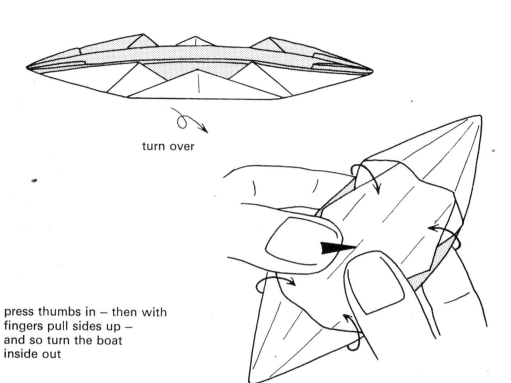

turn over

press thumbs in — then with
fingers pull sides up —
and so turn the boat
inside out

Sanbow

*A Japanese
offering tray*

*Begin with the
corners folded to
the centre*

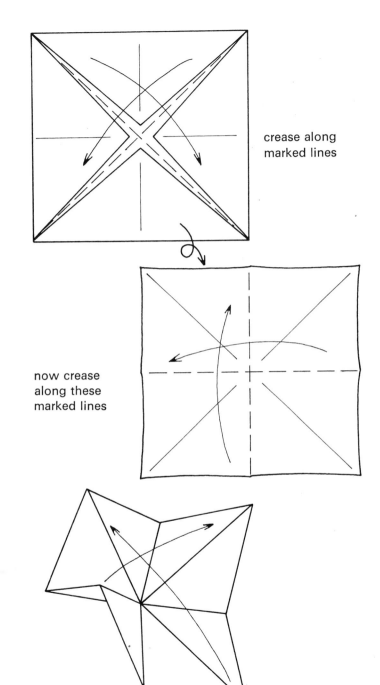

crease along
marked lines

now crease
along these
marked lines

pull the corners
together

42

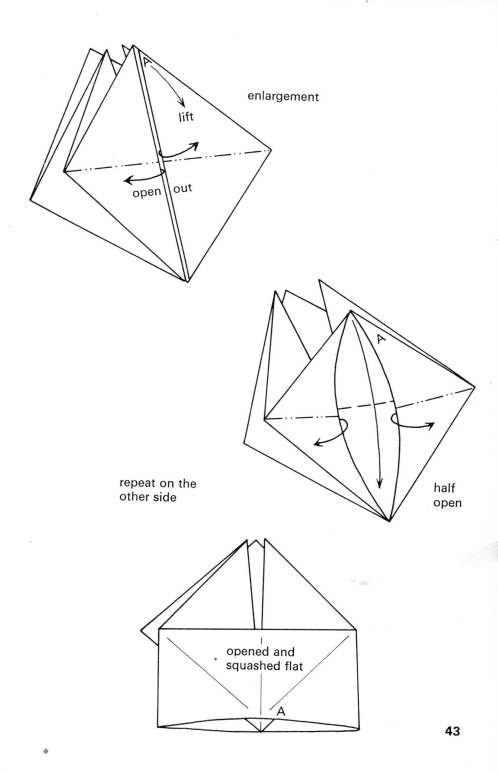

enlargement

lift

open out

repeat on the
other side

half
open

opened and
squashed flat

A

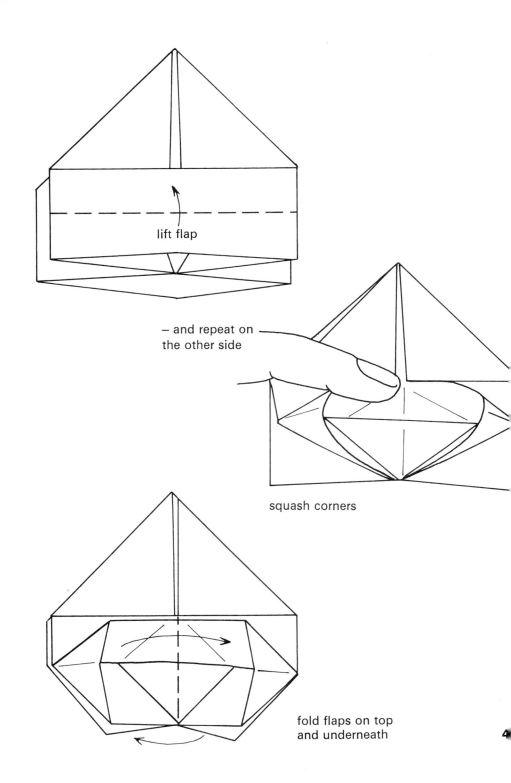

lift flap

– and repeat on
the other side

squash corners

fold flaps on top
and underneath

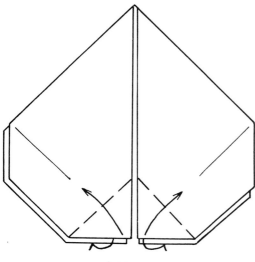

fold corners

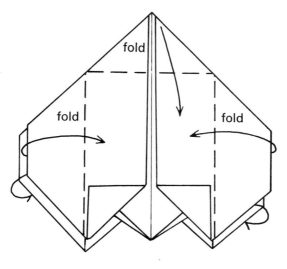

repeat behind

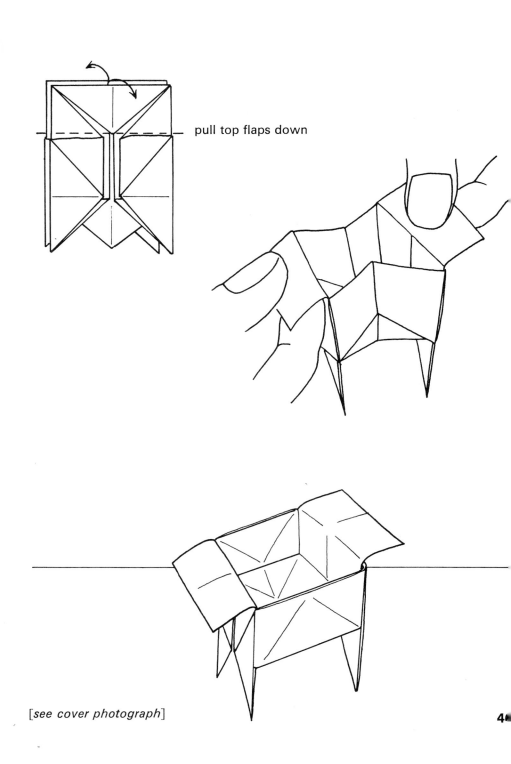

pull top flaps down

[see cover photograph]

Multiform

*This is a series
of standard folds*

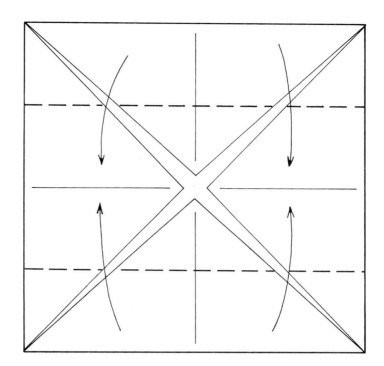

fold sides to middle

fold sides to middle

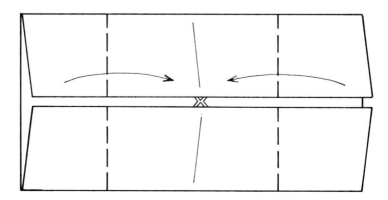

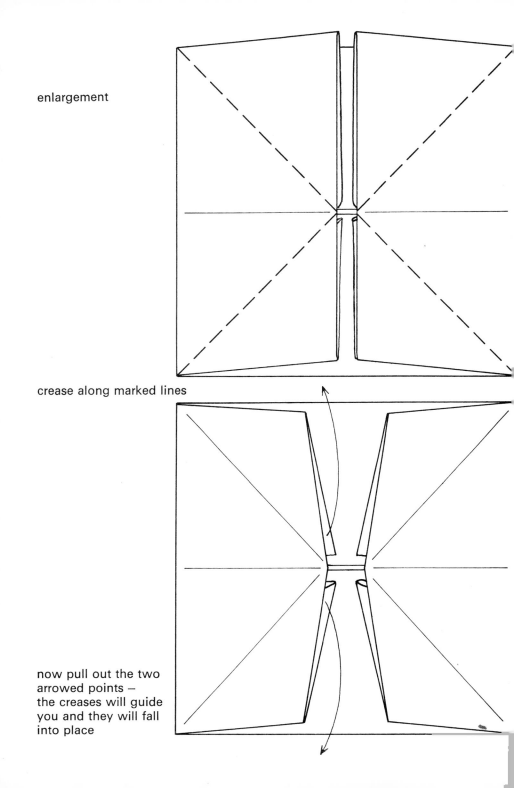

enlargement

crease along marked lines

now pull out the two
arrowed points –
the creases will guide
you and they will fall
into place

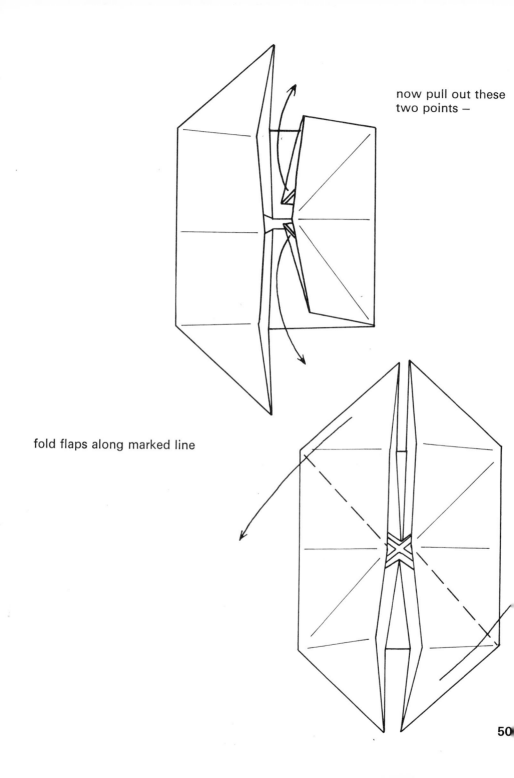

now pull out these
two points –

fold flaps along marked line

50

Windmill and vase

to make this windmill

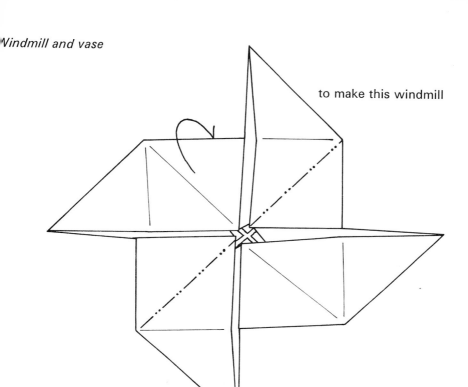

Fold the model in half backwards – to make this vase

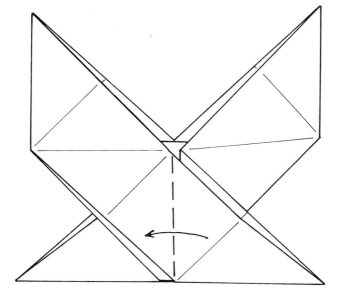

Now fold flap to make this boat with sail

[see next page]

51

Sailboat and catamaran

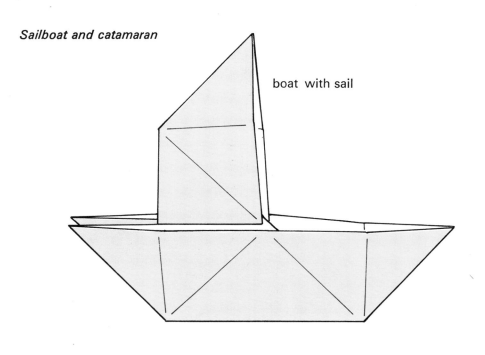

boat with sail

now start at bottom
of page 50
and fold the model
in half to make
this catamaran

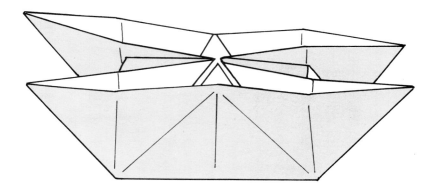

Bird Base

*This is the most
important base
in Origami*

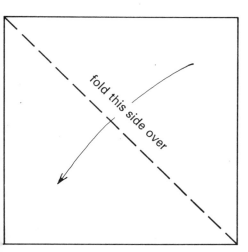

fold this side over

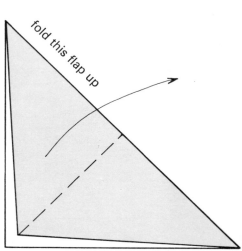

fold this flap up

squash this flap

enlargement

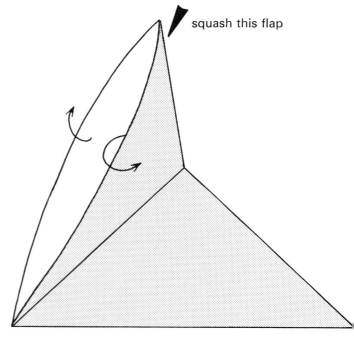

here the flap is
seen half squashed

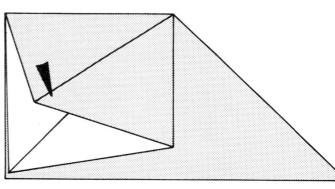

completely squashed

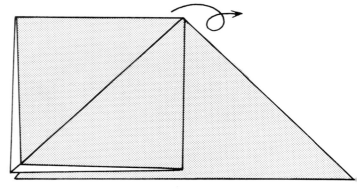

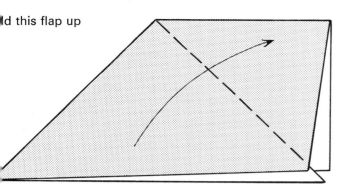

...d this flap up

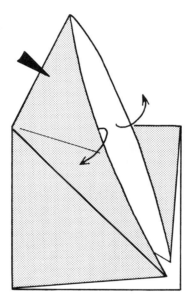

squash also

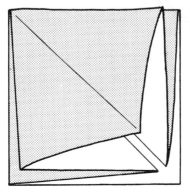

squashed

this is the
Preliminary Base

55

fold flaps along marked lines —
and the same behind

enlargement

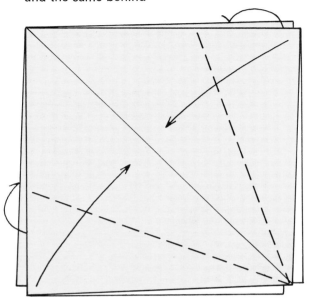

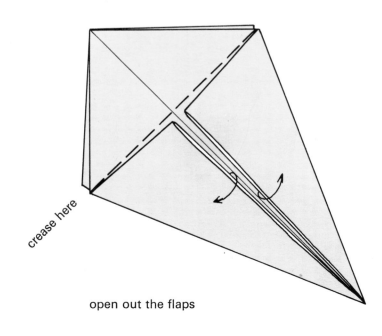

crease here

open out the flaps

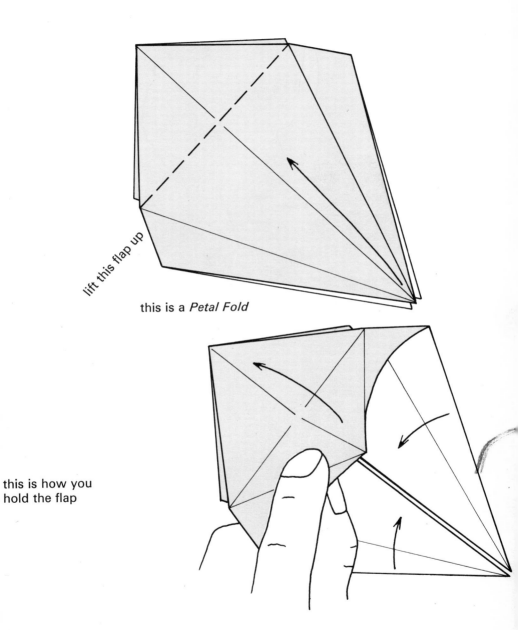

lift this flap up

this is a *Petal Fold*

this is how you
hold the flap

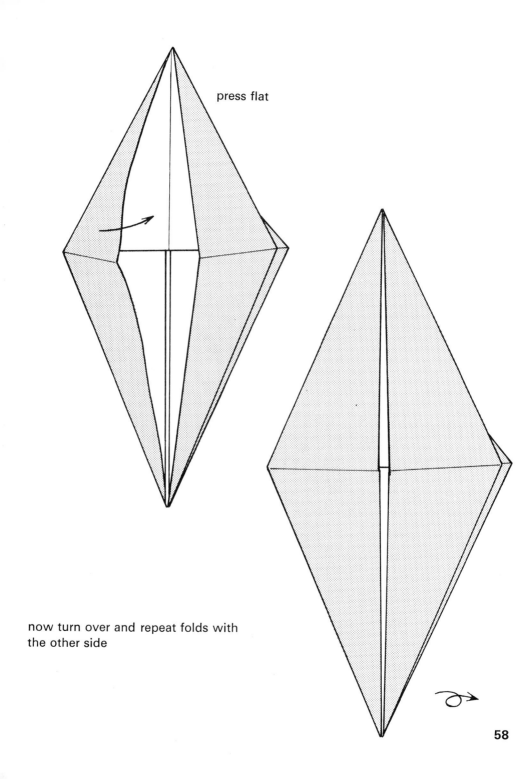

press flat

now turn over and repeat folds with
the other side

this is the *Bird Base*

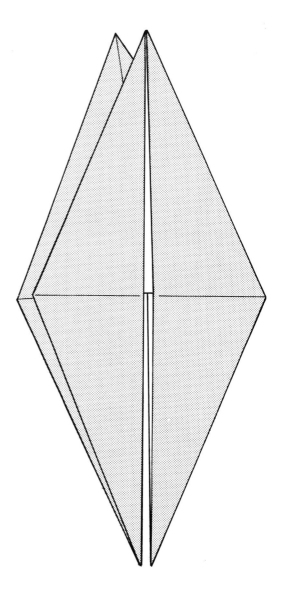

Beginning from the Bird Base,
you can make the Flapping
Bird, the Pigeon and the Swans
and can go on to invent more
models of your own

59

Flapping bird

*An ancient
Japanese fold*

Reverse Fold
this point —

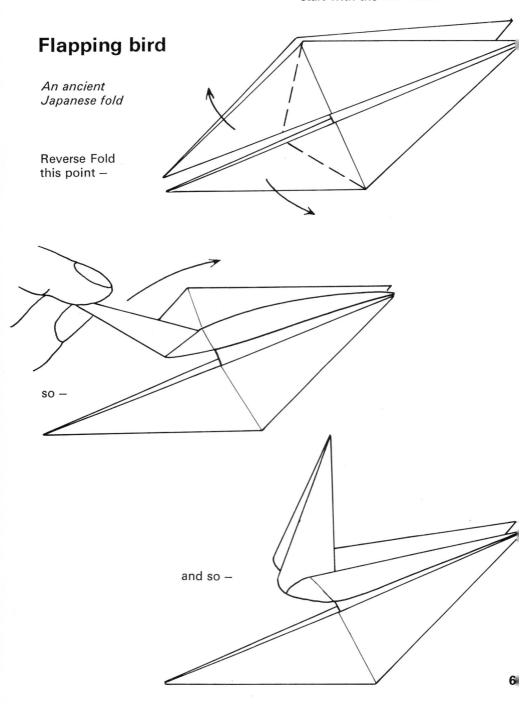

so —

and so —

6

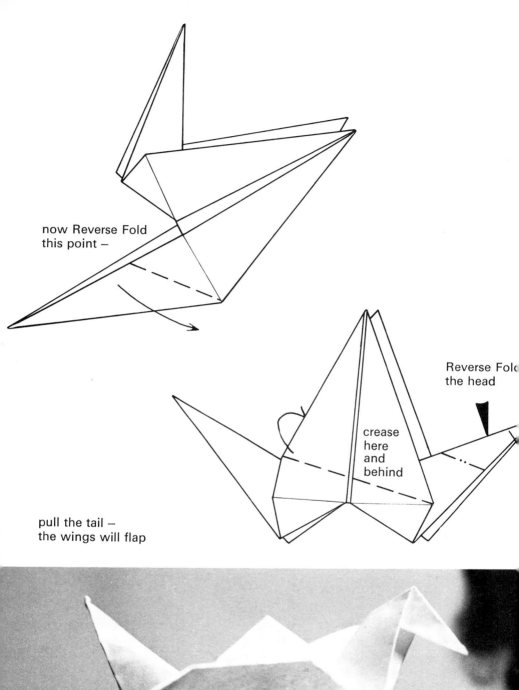

now Reverse Fold
this point –

Reverse Fold
the head

crease
here
and
behind

pull the tail –
the wings will flap

igeon

model by
kira Yoshizawa,
kyo, Japan

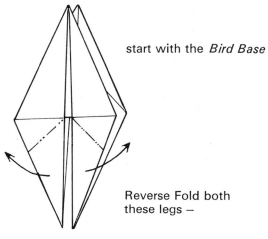

start with the *Bird Base*

Reverse Fold both
these legs —

but Reverse Fold
only as far as this

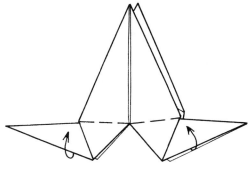

open up the leg flaps

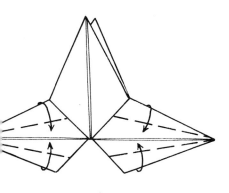

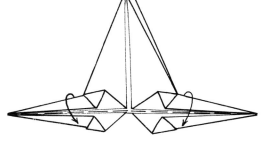

ld all four sides
the centre line
make legs —

now fold the top flaps
down to complete legs —

63

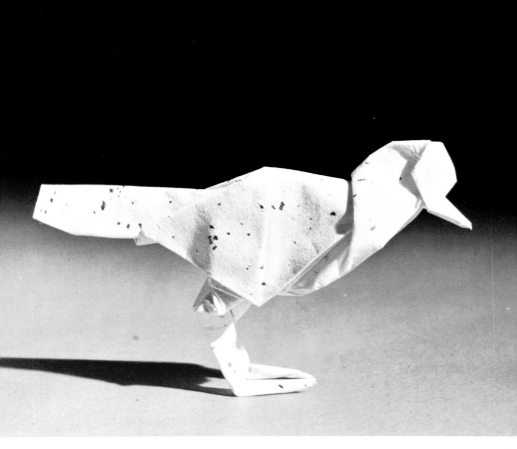

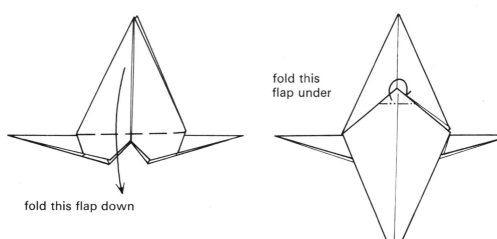

fold this
flap under

fold this flap down

6

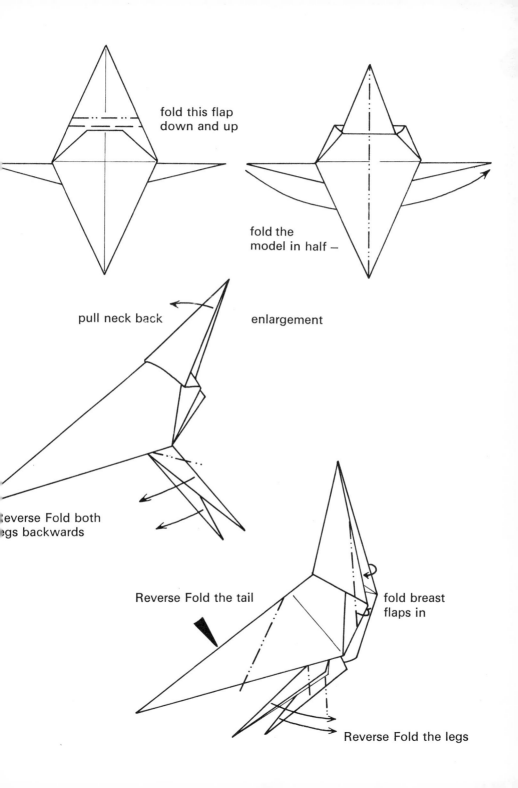

fold this flap
down and up

fold the
model in half —

pull neck back

enlargement

Reverse Fold both
legs backwards

Reverse Fold the tail

fold breast
flaps in

Reverse Fold the legs

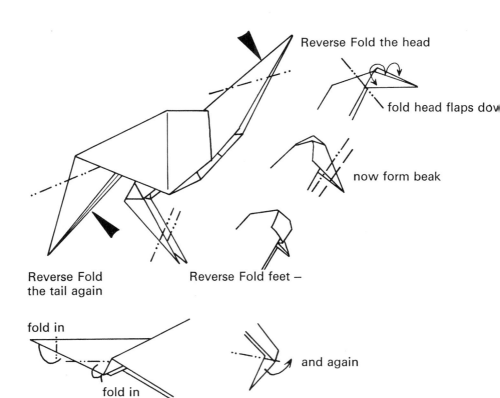

Reverse Fold the head

fold head flaps dow

now form beak

Reverse Fold
the tail again

Reverse Fold feet –

fold in

fold in

and again

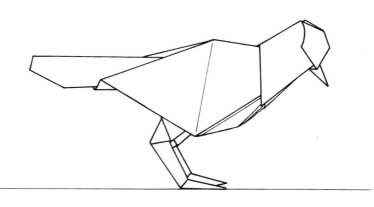

Frog

This model starts with the Preliminary Base

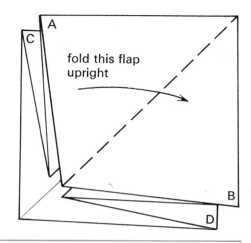

fold this flap upright

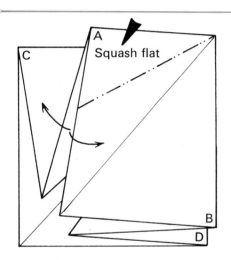

Squash flat

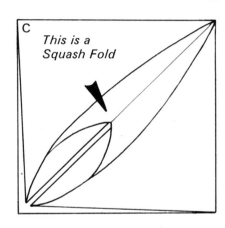

This is a Squash Fold

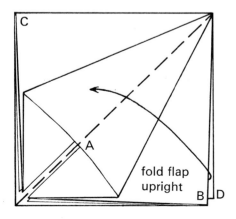

fold flap upright

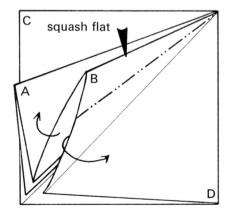

squash flat

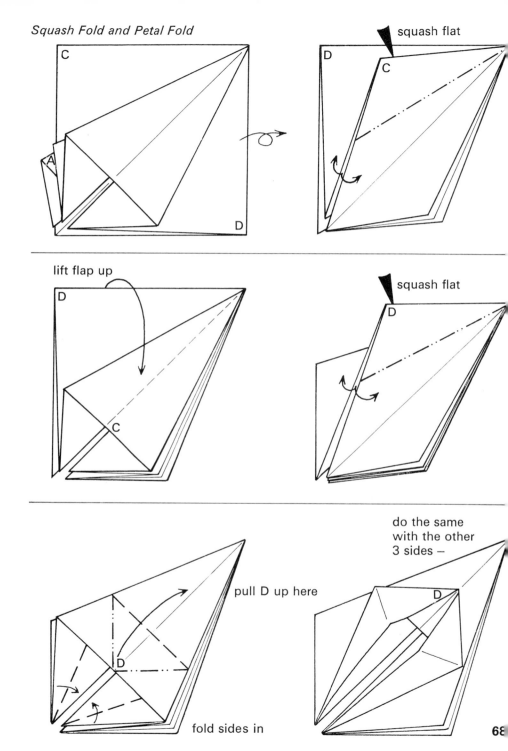

Squash Fold and Petal Fold

C

A

D

squash flat

D

C

lift flap up

D

C

squash flat

D

pull D up here

D

fold sides in

do the same
with the other
3 sides —

D

68

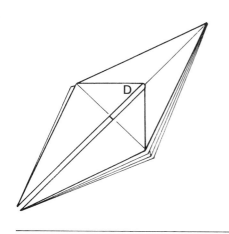

D

fold top flap
over

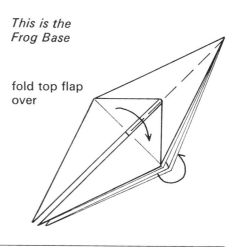

fold in

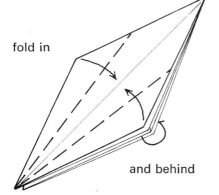

and behind

fold over

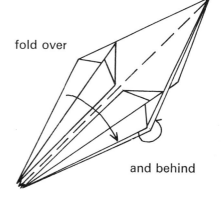

and behind

fold in

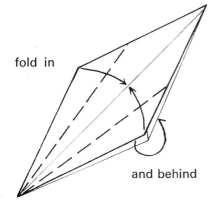

and behind

fold over

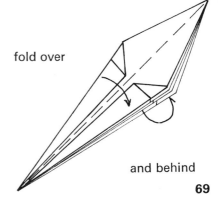

and behind

69

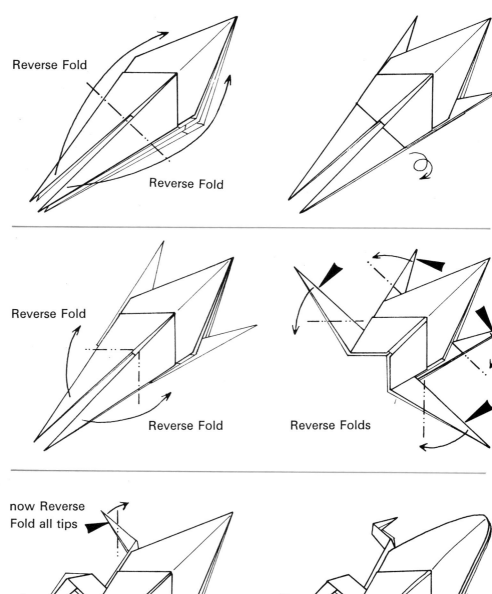

Reverse Fold

Reverse Fold

Reverse Fold

Reverse Fold

Reverse Folds

now Reverse
Fold all tips

blow

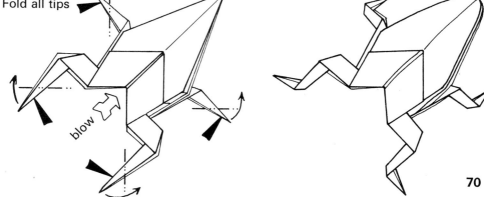

Penguins

*This model is by
Robert Harbin, England,
and uses the
Fish Base*

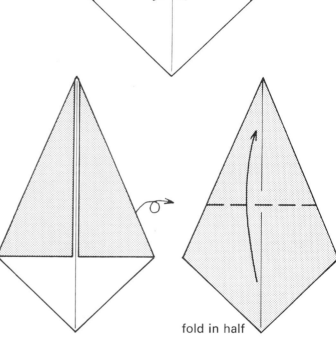

fold in half

pull down and flatten

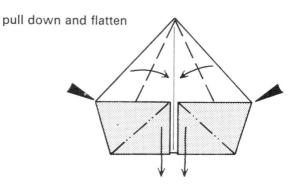

72

enlargement

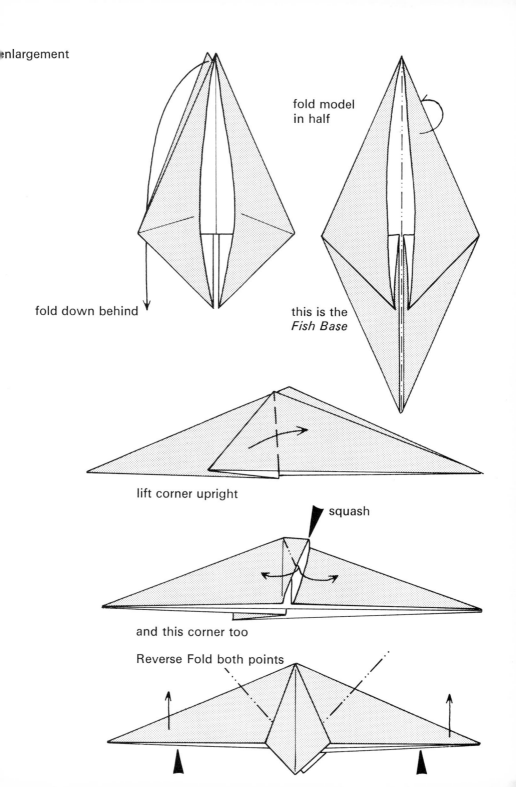

fold model
in half

fold down behind

this is the
Fish Base

lift corner upright

squash

and this corner too

Reverse Fold both points

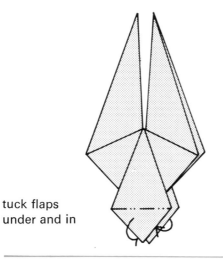

tuck flaps
under and in

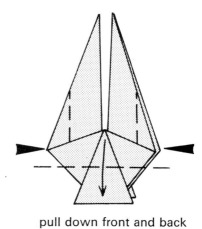

pull down front and back

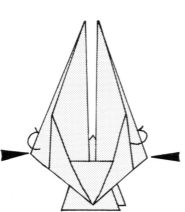

Reverse Fold points

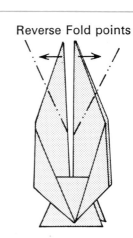

now form heads

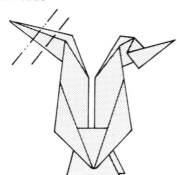

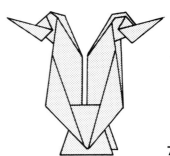

74

Penguin

*A fold by Eric Bird,
England, using a
Stretched Bird Base*

you are making a
Stretched Bird Base

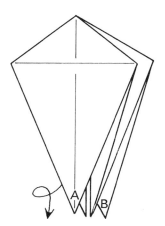

hold points A and B

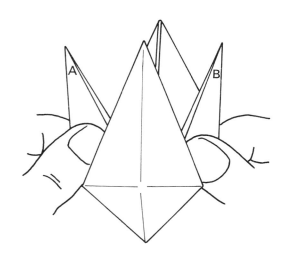

pull firmly

bring C and D together —
press flat

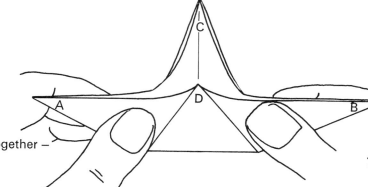

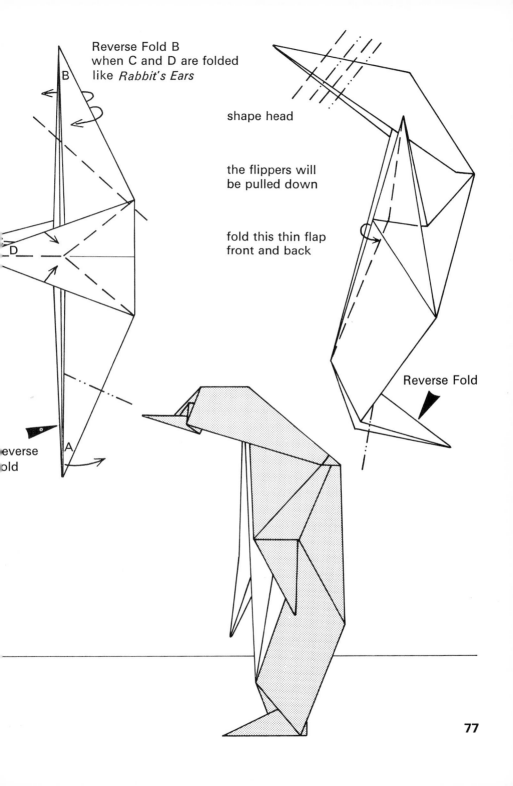

Reverse Fold B
when C and D are folded
like *Rabbit's Ears*

B

shape head

the flippers will
be pulled down

fold this thin flap
front and back

D

Reverse Fold

Reverse
Fold

A

77

Tropical bird

*A model by
Ligia Montoya,
Argentina,
using the
Fish Base*

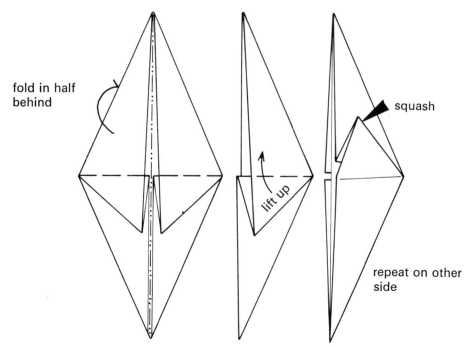

fold in half
behind

lift up

squash

repeat on other
side

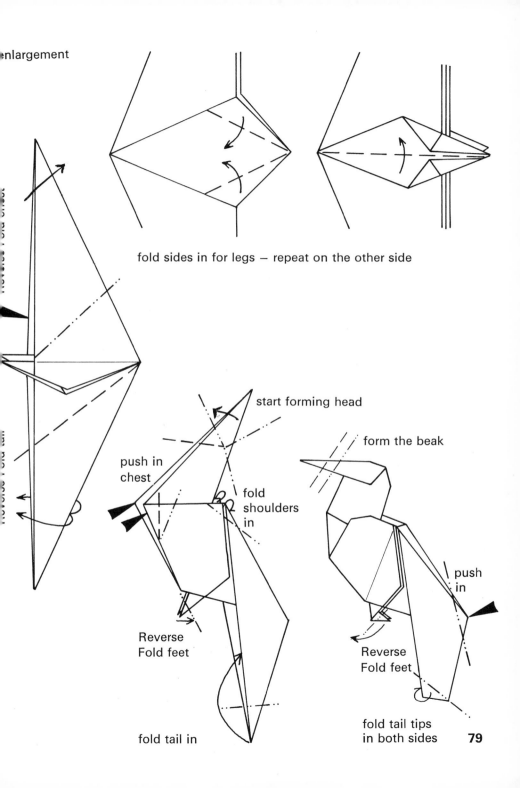

fold sides in for legs — repeat on the other side

push in
chest

start forming head

fold
shoulders
in

form the beak

push
in

Reverse
Fold feet

Reverse
Fold feet

fold tail in

fold tail tips
in both sides

79

Decoration

*Designed by
Robert Harbin,
England.
It begins with the
first five stages
of the Multiform*

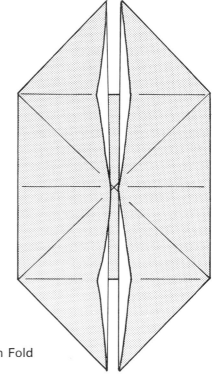

lift and Squash Fold
each corner

press flat

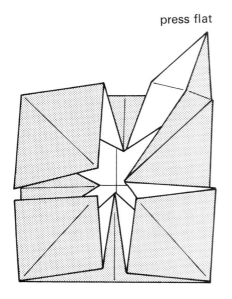

fold in eight flaps

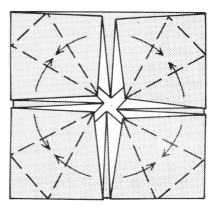

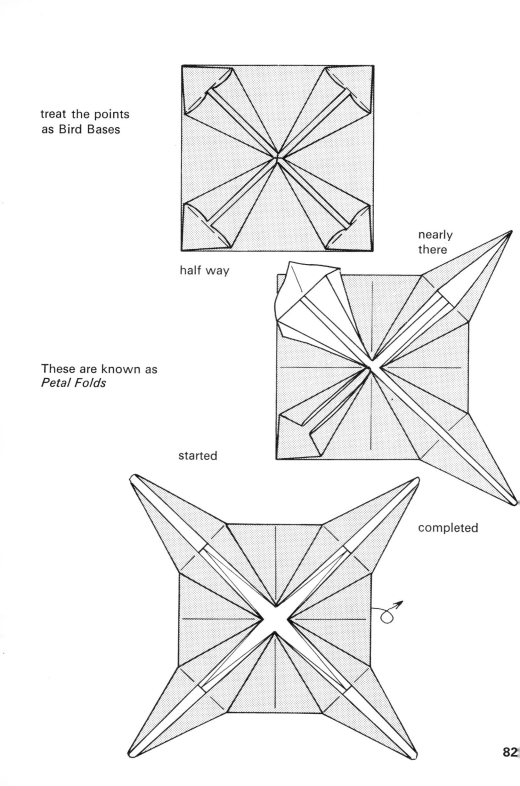

treat the points
as Bird Bases

half way

nearly
there

These are known as
Petal Folds

started

completed

82

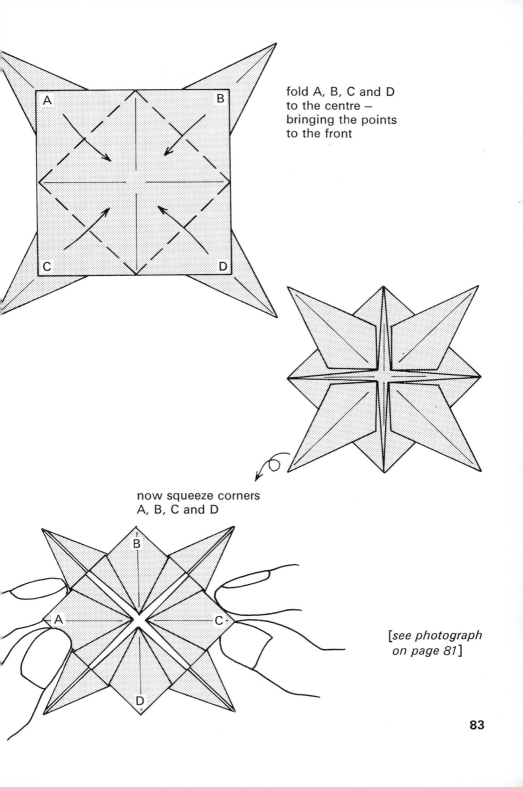

fold A, B, C and D
to the centre –
bringing the points
to the front

now squeeze corners
A, B, C and D

*[see photograph
on page 81]*

Ornithonimus

*A model by
Sidney French,
England*

form this
shape

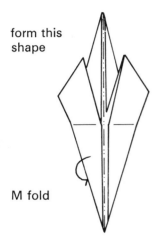

M fold

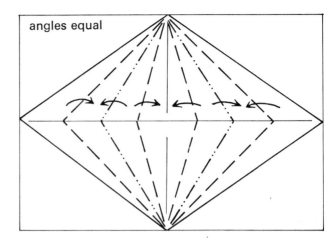

angles equal

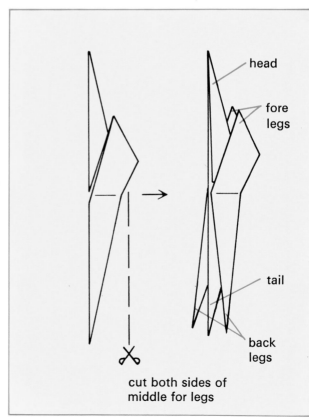

head

fore
legs

tail

back
legs

cut both sides of
middle for legs

the tail

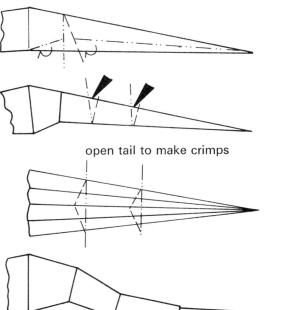

open tail to make crimps

the head and neck

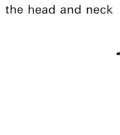

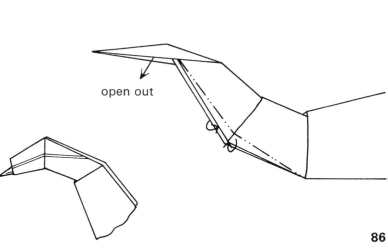

open out

86

back legs

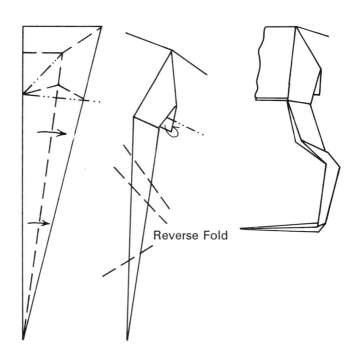

Reverse Fold

fore legs

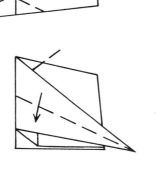

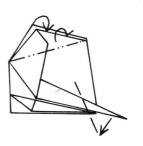

87

Swans

*A model by Tim Ward
and Trev Hatchett,
Oxford University.
Begin with a
Bird Base*

fold flaps
front and back

Reverse Fold
inside points either
side of middle point

Reverse Fold middle point

Squash Fold B and C

C
B
A

Reverse Fold
A and D

D

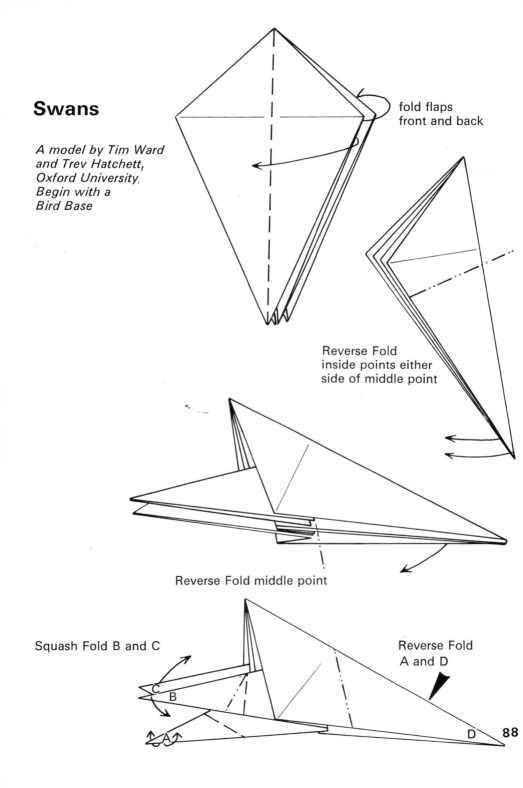

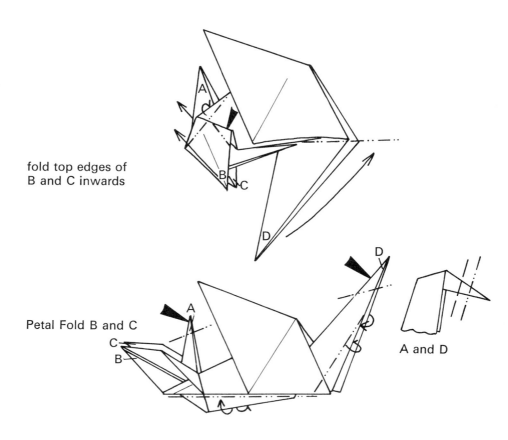

fold top edges of
B and C inwards

Petal Fold B and C

A and D

tuck in flaps to lock base

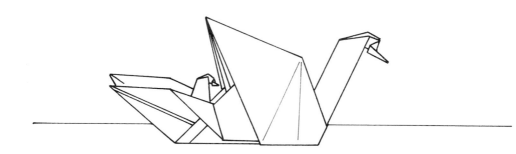

Books and materials

SOME SOURCES OF ORIGAMI PAPER AND BOOKS

The Art Department
Foyle's Book Shop
Charing Cross Road
London WC2

Melcombe Toys Ltd
23 Melcombe Street
London NW1

L. Davenport & Co.
51 Great Russell Street
London WC1

Charles E. Tuttle Company
Rutland
Vermont
USA

Mitsukiku
74a Lower Sloane Street
London SW1
and
18 Brighton Square
Brighton 1

Mrs Lillian Oppenheimer
The Origami Center
71 West Eleventh Street
New York 2 N.Y. USA

John Maxfield
9 The Broadway
Mill Hill
London NW7

The best Western publications on Origami are those of Harbin, Kenneway and Randlett; the best Japanese works are those of Nakano, Uchiyama and Yoshizawa.

HARBIN, ROBERT *Paper Magic*
   John Maxfield Ltd, 9 The Broadway, Mill Hill, London (1971 impression).
— *Origami 1: The Art of Paper-Folding*,
   The English Universities Press Ltd, London (1968); Hodder Paperbacks, London (1969).
— *Origami 2*, Hodder Paperbacks, London (1971).
— *Origami 3*, Hodder Paperbacks, London (1972).
— *Secrets of Origami*, Oldbourne Press, London (1963).

KENNEWAY, ERIC *Simple Origami*
   Dryad Press, Leicester (1970).
— *Origami in Action*, Dryad Press, Leicester (1972).
— *The Best of Origami: New Models by Contemporary Folders*,
   E. P. Dutton & Co., Inc., New York (1963).
— *The Flapping Bird: An Origami Monthly*. Published at $6.00 a year by Jay Marshall, 5082 N. Lincoln Ave, Chicago, Illinois 60625.

HONDA, ISAO *The World of Origami*
Japan Publications Trading Co., 1255 Howard Street, San
Francisco, California 94103 (1965).

KASAHARA, KUNIHIKO *Creative Origami*
Japan Publications Inc., Tokyo; distributed by Japan Publications
Trading Co., 1255 Howard Street, San Francisco, California 94103
(1968).

LEWIS, SHARI and OPPENHEIMER, LILLIAN *Folding Paper Puppet*
Stein and Day, New York (1962).
– *Folding Paper Toys*, Stein and Day, New York (1963).
– *Folding Paper Masks*, E. P. Dutton & Co., Inc., New York (1965).

SAKODA, JAMES MINORU *Modern Origami*
Simon and Schuster, New York (1969).

VAN BREDA, AART *Paper Folding and Modelling*
Faber and Faber, London (1965).

See Robert Harbin's *Secrets of Origami* for a more comprehensive
bibliography.